Bible
Prophecy
made
easy

Mark Water

P9-APY-987

HENDRICKSON
PUBLISHERS

Bible Prophecy Made Easy
Hendrickson Publishers, Inc.
P.O. Box 3473
Peabody, Massachusetts 01961-3473

Copyright © 1998 Hunt & Thorpe
Text copyright © 1998 Mark Water

ISBN 1-56563-369-5

Original edition published in
English under the title *"Bible Study
Made Easy"* by Hunt & Thorpe,
Alresford, Hants, UK.

Designed and produced
by Tony Cantale Graphics

All rights reserved. Except for
brief quotations in critical articles
or reviews, no part of this book
may be reproduced in any manner without
prior written permission from the publishers.

The right of Mark Water to be identified
as the author of this work has been asserted
by him in accordance with the Copyright
Designs and Patent Act 1988.

First printing — April 1998

Manufactured In Hong Kong / China

Unless otherwise noted, Scripture
quotations are taken from HOLY
BIBLE, NEW INTERNATIONAL
VERSION copyright © 1973, 1978,
1984 by International Bible
Society. All rights reserved.

Photography supplied by
Goodshoot, Digital Vision and
Tony Cantale

Illustrations by
Tony Cantale Graphics

Contents

Special pull-out chart
A bird's-eye view of Bible prophets

False prophecies

"It is not for you to know"

The burning question on the lips of the disciples of Jesus was, "Lord, are you at this time going to restore the kingdom of Israel?" The risen Jesus answered them qute clearly, "It is not for you to know the times or dates the Father has set by his own authority." *Acts 1:6-7*

But from the numerous confident predictions about the exact date of Jesus' return, you would think that Jesus had never said the above words.

Watch out for millennium predictions

If the last millennium is anything to go by, we can expect countless predictions about the end of the world, linked in some way to the year 2000.

5

PAST PREDICTIONS

• **1000** As the year 999 came to an end, crowds of crying people pushed their way into the old basilica of St Peter's in Rome, expecting the end of the world to occur as the dawn of the new millennium was ushered in.

• **1528** Hans Nut, a German bookbinder and self-declared prophet, claimed that the world would come to an end in 1528.

• **1933** According the respected Bible teacher Oswald J. Smith, in his book *Is the Antichrist at Hand?*, "the great tribulation, revival of the Roman empire, reign of Antichrist, and the battle of Armageddon must take place before the year 1933."

• **1988** If you had contributed $5 in 1988 to Ministries Inc., Montgomery, Alabama, you could have received a book by Rev. Colin Deal entitled *Christ Returns by 1988 – 101 Reasons Why.*

Six false prophecies about Jesus' return

False claims

As far back as the days of the New Testament, people were making false claims about the time of Jesus' return, and events linked to it.

Paul warned: "Do not become easily unsettled or alarmed by some prophecy, false report or letter supposed to have come from us, saying that the Day of the Lord has already come." *2 Thessalonians 2:2*

1. THE BIRTH OF THE ANTICHRIST

Before the end of the fourth century, Martin of Tours confidently stated that the Antichrist had already been born.

2. THE DESTRUCTION OF THE ROMAN PAPACY

Some Christians have identified certain prophecies in the Book of Revelation with Rome, the center of Roman Catholicism. Joachim prophesied, way back in the thirteenth century, that the papacy in Rome would be utterly destroyed in 1260.

3. THE DATE OF THE BATTLE OF ARMAGEDDON

The spiritual leader of the Lighthouse Gospel Tract Foundation, Maupin, predicted that:
- The rapture would take place before July, 1981.
- Satan would appear before December 1984.
- Satan would rule the world until May 14, 1988.
- The battle of Armageddon would take place on May 14, 1988.

4. THE DATE OF THE RAPTURE

The word "rapture" refers to the act of transferring a person from earth to heaven. It specifically refers to Christians being united with Jesus at his second coming: "After that, we who are still alive and are left will be caught up together with them in the clouds to meet the Lord in the air." *1 Thessalonians 4:17*

- A writer, using the pen name "Ted," in *Deadline 1981, Mockers Beware, Vol. 1*, declared that the rapture was about to arrive in August 1980, or at the latest by June 20, 1981.
- According to Dr. Charles Taylor, the rapture was to take place on September 25, 1975.
- October 28, 1992 was the predicted date for the rapture, according to an undated tract, not attributed to a named author, entitled *Mission For The Coming Days*, Orange County Division, Orange County, CA.

5. THE MORMON PREDICTION

The founder of the Mormons, Joseph Smith, predicted that the second coming of Jesus would take place before the end of 1891.

6. THE SEVENTH DAY ADVENTIST PREDICTION

The Seventh Day Adventist, William Miller, predicted that Jesus would finally return between March 21, 1843 and March 21, 1844.

Zeal is not enough

It is easy to be taken in by the enthusiasm of false prophets. Paul once described the misplaced enthusiasm of the Jews: "They are zealous... but their zeal is not based on knowledge." *Romans 10:2*

"Don't believe them"

Jesus said, "If anyone says to you, 'Look, here is the Christ!' or 'There he is!' do not believe it." *Matthew 24:23*

What did Jesus teach about the end of the world?

Jesus will return when the end of the world comes.

The promise

The personal return of Jesus is sometimes called his "second coming." While these two words "second coming" do not appear in the Bible, the event is mentioned about 300 times in the New Testament.

At Jesus' ascension, two angels told Jesus' disciples: "This same Jesus, who has been taken from you into heaven, will come back in the same way you have seen him go into heaven." *Acts 1:11*

Where can I read about Jesus coming again?

Gospels	Letters	Revelation
Matthew 19:28; 23:39; 24:1-51 *Mark 13:24-37* *Luke 12:35-48; 21:25-28*	*Romans 11:25-27* *1 Corinthians 11:26; 15:15-58* *1 Thessalonians 4:13-18* *2 Thessalonians 1:7-10* *2 Peter 3:10-12*	*Revelation 16:15* *Revelation 19:11-21*

"The sun will be darkened, and the moon will not give us light; the stars will fall from the sky, and the heavenly bodies will be shaken."
Mark 13:24-25

"For the Lord himself will come down from heaven, with a loud command, with the voice of the archangel and with the trumpet call of God, and the dead in Christ will rise first."
1 Thessalonians 4:16

"But the beast was captured, and with the false prophet who had performed the miraculous signs on his behalf."
Revelation 19:20

When, exactly, will Jesus return?

Many godly people have studied the biblical prophecies and identified some of the events which will take place before Jesus' return, from which they have concluded that Jesus' second coming is imminent. *See Luke 21:8-12.*

Events associated with the time of Jesus' return are:

• War	• Rumors of war	• Revolution
• Earthquake	• Famine	• Pestilence
• Great signs from heaven	• Persecution of God's followers	

Some people have been rash enough to predict the year, the time of day and the place of Jesus' return. Every prediction has shown the fallibility, the inaccuracy, and the presumptuousness of human beings.

Others say that God will give no signs, and that nobody knows the day or the hour when Jesus will return. Jesus will return when he is least expected. *See Matthew 24:36-44.*

The gospel will be preached throughout the world

> "And this gospel of the kingdom will be preached in the whole world as a testimony to all nations, and then the end will come." *Matthew 24:14*

The Bible has been translated into over 2,000 languages and dialects, and the Christian message has been sent throughout the world by radio, TV, and on the Internet. Therefore, many believe that this prophecy has already been fulfilled.

There may be a long time to wait

By referring to certain parables, some people have concluded that many years have yet to pass before Jesus returns:

- "My master is staying away a long time."
  (The parable of the wicked servant.) *Matthew 24:48*
- "The bridegroom was a long time in coming."
  (The parable of the ten virgins.) *Matthew 25:5*
- "After a long time the master ...."
  (The parable of the talents.) *Matthew 25:19*

To think over

- Some would consider that this verse from 2 Peter 3:8 is an argument against Jesus' return being a long way away:
  "With the Lord a day is like a thousand years, and a thousand years are like a day."

What are the "signs" of the end of the world?

Bible prophecy has predicted that certain events will take place before Jesus returns.

There will be more false prophets

• "The Spirit clearly says that in later times some will abandon the faith and follow deceiving spirits and things taught by demons."
1 Timothy 4:1

• "But there were also false prophets among the people, just as there will be false teachers among you."
2 Peter 1:2

There will be global distress on an unprecedented scale

This will include natural disasters.

• "There will be a time of distress such as has not happened from the beginning of nations until then." *Daniel 12:1*

• "The great Day of the Lord is near – near and coming quickly. ...a day of trouble and ruin, a day of darkness and gloom, a day of clouds and blackness."
Zephaniah 1:14-15

Some people will be unprepared and some will lose their faith

• "In the last days scoffers will come, scoffing and following their own evil desires. They will say, 'Where is this coming he promised? Ever since our fathers died, everything goes on as it has since the beginning of creation.'"
2 Peter 3:3-4

Many Christians will be expecting Jesus' return

It will be just like Jesus' first coming, when people such as John the Baptist, Anna and Simeon, were waiting for Jesus to appear.

• "While we wait for the blessed hope – the glorious appearing of our great God and Savior, Jesus Christ."
Titus 2:13

Believers will be transformed

Those who are alive at Jesus' return will not die but will be transformed.

• "We who are still alive and are left will be caught up together with them in the clouds to meet the Lord in the air. And so we will be with the Lord for ever."
1 Thessalonians 4:17

Satan's opposition to Jesus and his kingdom will be at its height

• "Don't let anyone deceive you in any way, for that day will not come until the rebellion occurs and the man of lawlessness is revealed, the man doomed to destruction. He will oppose and exalt himself over everything that is called God or is worshiped, so that he sets himself up in God's Temple, proclaiming to be God."
2 Thessalonians 2:3-4

The battle of Armageddon

The Bible states the name and place of the final conflict between God and Satan. It is the Plain of Esdraelon, which runs from the port of Haifa on the coast of Israel to the River Jordan.

• "Then they gathered the kings together to the place that in Hebrew is called Armageddon."
Revelation 16:16

Are we in the "last days"?

The "last days" are the final period of human history. In the sense that the Christian era is the last great epoch before God ends the world, we are already in the "last days."

Millenarianism is the belief that there will be a future millennium preceding Christ's return, during which time he will reign in peace. It is based on Revelation 20. Christian views on how and when the millennium will take place follow three main interpretations: amillennial, postmillenial, and premillennial.

The amillennial interpretation

The amillennial view interprets Revelation 20:7-10 in a spiritual, rather than a literal, way.

- The thousand years means an indefinite period of time, not literally one thousand years, between the death of Christ and his return.
- Satan will be bound before Jesus' appearance. Jesus will appear without warning.
- The covenant relationship promised to Israel is inherited by the Church in a spiritual way.
- The "first resurrection" is when people go from death to life by

The millennium vision in the Bible

The thousand years

And I saw an angel coming down out of heaven, having the key to the Abyss and holding in his hand a great chain. He seized the dragon, that ancient serpent, who is the Devil, or Satan, and bound him for a thousand years. He threw him into the Abyss, and locked and sealed it over him, to keep him from deceiving the nations any more until the thousand years were ended. After that, he must be set free for a short time.

I saw thrones on which were seated those who had been given authority to judge. And I saw the souls of those who had been beheaded because of their testimony for Jesus and because of the word of God. They had not worshiped the beast or his image and had not received his mark on their foreheads or their hands. They came to life and reigned with Christ for a thousand years. (The rest of the dead did not come to life until the thousand years were ended.) This is the first resurrection. Blessed and holy are

becoming Christians. They reign with Christ in death. The "rest of the dead" are the non-Christians who will come to life to face judgment.

those who have part in the first resurrection. The second death has no power over them, but they will be priests of God and of Christ and will reign with him for a thousand years. *Revelation 20:1-6*

Satan's doom

When the thousand years are over, Satan will be released from his prison and will go out to deceive the nations in the four corners of the earth – Gog and Magog [the nations of the world as they unite for a final assault on God] – to gather them for battle. In number they are like the sand on the seashore. They marched across the breadth of the earth and surrounded the camp of God's people, the city he loves. But fire came down from heaven and devoured them. And the Devil, who deceived them, was thrown into the lake of burning sulphur, where the beast and the false prophet had been thrown. They will be tormented day and night for ever and ever. *Revelation 20:7-10*

The postmillennial interpretation

This view suggests that there will be a literal thousand years during which the Church will be very active.
• The preaching of the gospel will usher in the millennium.

• A time of spiritual growth will come before the end.
• Jesus' return will be after the millennium, when judgment takes place.

The premillennial interpretation

This interpretation assumes that Revelation 20 is referring to an actual future event.
• The Antichrist will rise to power.
• Jesus will appear, in bodily form, before the millennium.
• Jesus will reign on earth for a thousand years in peace and righteousness.
• Satan will lead a rebellion at the end of the thousand years, which Jesus will defeat.
• The day of judgment follows the final battle between good and evil, the world is destroyed and a new earth and heaven are created.

Points of agreement

While Christians differ over points of detail, they agree on the following basic beliefs about the future:
• Jesus will return.
• Jesus' "saints" (faithful followers) will be resurrected.
• It will be a time of judgment for sinners and sin.

Who is the "beast" of the Book of Revelation?

Hostile powers were often called "beasts" in prophetic imagery. In Revelation 13, two beasts are mentioned, one coming out of the sea and one out of the earth.

The beast from the sea

Read Revelation 13:1-8. The beast emerges from the sea, which the Jews thought of as an evil place. The beast appears to be an amalgamation of the four beasts mentioned in Daniel 7. Its crown and horns (which stand for power and sovereignty) illustrate its clear defiance of God and represent an authoritarian, anti-God State.

The prophecies from the Book of Daniel shed light on the beasts of Revelation 13.

Daniel and his prophecies

The Book of Daniel contains prophecies of future events, given to Daniel. The prophecies in Daniel chapters two, seven and eight were fulfilled during the Babylonian empire, the Medeo-Persian empire, the Grecian empire, and the Roman empire.

Fulfilled prophecy in the Book of Daniel
Dreams and visions

Empires	Large statue 2:32-45	Four beasts 7	Ram and goat 8
Babylonian	Head of gold 2:32, 37-38	A lion 7:4	A ram 8:3-4, 20
Medeo-Persian	Chest and arms of silver 2:32, 39	A bear 7:5	A goat with one horn 8:5-8, 21
Greek	Bronze belly and thighs 2:32, 39	A leopard 7:6	A goat with four horns 8:8, 22
Roman	Legs of iron, feet of iron and clay 2:32, 40-41	A strong beast 7:7, 11, 19, 23	A goat with little horn 8:9-14

Daniel and the Antichrist

Differing interpretations have been given to the prophecies in the Book of Daniel. For example, people who strongly emphasize that Daniel's prophecies relate to the last days, see references to the Antichrist in the iron of chapter two, the horns of chapter seven, and the little horn of chapter eight.

The beast from the earth

"Then I saw another beast, coming out of the earth. He had two horns like a lamb, but he spoke like a dragon. ... He ... forced everyone, small and great, rich and poor, free and slave, to receive a mark on his right hand or on his forehead, so that no one could buy or sell unless he had the mark, which is the name of the beast or the number of his name." "This calls for wisdom. If anyone has insight, let him calculate the number of the beast, for it is man's number. His number is 666." *Revelation 13:11, 16-18*

The beast from the earth is usually taken to represent religious authority. The background to this vision was the practice of emperor worship, and the worship of Caesar as a divine being. The beast from the earth could "cause all who refused to worship the image to be killed." *Revelation 13:15*

15

What about 666?

The mysterious number, **666**, revealed in Revelation 13:18, has generated numerous interpretations, including some very bizarre ones.

• Two favorite interpretations rely on **666** being a code for a particular word or group of words. The letters of the alphabet are given numerical values, and so the letters making up a person's name will have a numerical total. Working back from the number **666**, this reveals the Hebrew words "Nero-Caesar."

• In a similar way, the value of the Greek letters spelling the name of Domitian, the third emperor of Rome, was also calculated to be

666. This was gleaned from the words "Emperor Caesar Domitian Augustus Germanicus" on a coin circulating in the province of Asia, which gave the required total of **666**.

• John, the writer of the Book of Revelation, may have used the number **666** as a code, rather than risking arrest for sedition by using a ruler's name.

• Others have suggested that the number seven stands for perfection, or even for God himself. The number six stands for imperfection, and the number **666** stands for total imperfection – that is, a philosophy or person that equals total imperfection or is anti-God.

When will the prophecies of Revelation come true?

Many of the prophecies of the Bible, and especially the prophetic themes of the Old Testament, are found in the Book of Revelation.

Great prophetic themes found in Revelation

Theme	Reference in Revelation	Other references
Paradise lost, paradise regained	Revelation 21-22	Genesis 3
The Antichrist	Revelation 13:1-10; 19:20	Ezekiel 28:1-10
The Lord Jesus Christ	Revelation 1:1	Genesis 3:15
The times of the Gentiles	Revelation 6:1-19:16	Daniel 2:37-44
The Church	Revelation 2-3	Matthew 16:18
The great tribulation	Revelation 4-19	Deuteronomy 4:29-30
The nations judged	Revelation 16:13-16	Joel 3:1-10
The second coming of Jesus	Revelation 19:11-16	Zechariah 14:1-14
The wicked judged	Revelation 20:11-15	Psalm 9:17
The new heaven and earth	Revelation 21-22	Isaiah 65:17

New heavens and a new earth

Behold, I will create new heavens and a new earth, The former things will not be remembered, nor will they come to mind.
Isaiah 65:17

Then I saw a new heaven and a new earth, for the first heaven and the first earth had passed away, and there was no longer any sea. I saw the Holy City, the new Jerusalem, coming down out of heaven from God, prepared as a bride beautifully dressed for her husband.
Revelation 21:1-2

Look up the references on the chart. See how the prophecies were fulfilled in the Book of Revelation.

Four ways to interpret the Book of Revelation

The answer to the question "When will the prophecies of the book of Revelation come true?" depends on how you interpret this book. There are four main approaches.

• The preterist view
The Book of Revelation was meant for Christians of the first century, who would have known exactly what it meant. We would expect to find limited revelations about our own times.

• The historic view
The Book of Revelation outlines the history of the Western world from the first century to our own.

• The futurist view
The Book of Revelation refers exclusively to the end of the world, and contains no historical allusions.

• The symbolic or spiritual view
The Book of Revelation is full of symbols. Each symbol should not necessarily be linked up with world history, but is written to encourage Christians in basic spiritual principles.

Which view is correct?
No one view is totally satisfying.
- The preterist view means that the Book of Revelation is past history with only encouraging principles for today.
- The futurist view only applies to Christians living at the end of time.
- A combination of the historic view and the symbolic view has much to commend it.

Two fulfillments
Many prophecies in the Bible have two points of reference. They refer to their own day and they point forward to a future fulfillment. The prophecy in Isaiah 7:14 about a young woman, for example, was true in Isaiah's day, and it also refers to Mary, Jesus' mother. The prophecies in the Book of Revelation refer both to their own time, (probably the times of persecution under Domitian, AD 81-96) and to the events at the end of time.

See also: *How to study Revelation*, page 18.

How to study Revelation

The Book of Revelation remains a closed book for many. When it is opened, it is found to be full of startling, and sometimes frightening, images and symbols. Nobody should be put off by these: they offer clues to the understanding of this book.

Number seven
Number seven is the key which unlocks the meaning of the Book of Revelation. The whole book is built on a framework of the number seven.

The seven churches	*Revelation 2:1-3:22*
• The seven churches	*Revelation 1:4, 2:1, 8, 12, 18; 3:1, 7, 14*
• The seven spirits	*Revelation 1:4*
• The seven lampstands	*Revelation 1:12*
• The seven stars	*Revelation 1:16*
The seven seals	*Revelation 5:1*
The seven horns	*Revelation 5:6*
The seven angels	*Revelation 8:2*
The seven trumpets	*Revelation 8:2*
The seven thunders	*Revelation 10:3*
The seven personages	*Revelation 12:1-13:18*
• The woman	Revelation 12:1-2
•The dragon	*Revelation 12:3-4*
• The man child	*Revelation 12:5*
• The archangel Michael	*Revelation 12:7*
• The remnant	*Revelation 12:17*
• The beast from the sea	*Revelation 13:1-8*
• The beast from the earth	*Revelation 13:11-18*
The seven last plagues	*Revelation 15:1-16:21*
The seven golden bowls	*Revelation 15:7*
The seven kings	*Revelation 17:10*

The seven new things in the Book of Revelation
Seven stands for perfection and completeness.

• New heavens	*Revelation 21:1*
• New earth	*Revelation 21:1*
• New city	*Revelation 21:9-23*
• New nations	*Revelation 21:24-27*
• New river	*Revelation 22:1*
• New tree	*Revelation 22:2*
• New throne	*Revelation 22:3-5*

• See also: *When will the prophecies of Revelation come true?*, page 16.

The thousand years — the millennium

What is the millennium?

The millennium is the name given to the thousand years mentioned in Revelation 20:2-7. It is the time of the reign of Jesus and his followers over the earth. Christian views on how and when the millennium will take place follow three main interpretations: amillennial, postmillennial, and premillennial.

Amillennial

Not literally a thousand years.

The thousand years may be fulfilled in heaven or in the age of the Church.

Before Jesus comes, Satan will be bound. This view rejects the idea of a future millennium.

Then will follow: the destruction of the world, the Day of Judgment, the creation of a new earth and new heaven.

(Supported by Augustine, Milligan and Berkhof)

Postmillennial	Premillennial	0
The thousand years will start with global gospel preaching. It will be the age of the Spirit, a time of spiritual prosperity for the Church on earth.	Before the thousand years, the Antichrist will be powerful.	
During the thousand years, there will be a great response to Jesus and the kingdom of God will be established on earth.	Before the thousand years, Jesus will come and will be seen by all. Jesus will usher in a thousand-year reign of peace and righteousness.	
At the end of the thousand years Christ will return to earth.	At the end of the thousand years, Satan will rebel, and Jesus will defeat him.	
Then will follow: the destruction of the world, the Day of Judgment, the creation of a new earth and a new heaven.	Then will follow: the destruction of the world, the Day of Judgment, the creation of a new earth and new heaven.	21
(Supported by Fairbairn and Warfield)	(Supported by Schofield, Ryrie and Walvoord)	1000

Who is the "Antichrist"?

Some Bible commentators have had no difficulty in attempting to identify the Antichrist. Names that have been suggested over the years range from Nero to Hitler, the Pope, Saddam Hussein and Henry Kissinger.

Who is the Antichrist?

- The Antichrist is someone who opposes Christ.

- He is an evil person.

- At the end of the world he is going to head a rebellion against Christ.

John defines the Antichrist

John identifies for us the main characteristic of the Antichrist: "It is the man who denies that Jesus is the Christ. Such a man is the Antichrist – he denies the Father and the Son." *1 John 2:22*

John tells us that there will be more than one Antichrist: "Even now many Antichrists have come." *1 John 2:18*

Characteristics of the Antichrist

Although the Antichrist is not Satan himself, he is like Satan in many ways.

• He denies that Jesus is really God.
"Every spirit that acknowledges that Jesus Christ has come in the flesh is from God, but every spirit that does not acknowledge Jesus is not from God. This is the spirit of the Antichrist."
1 John 4:2-3

• He denies the Father.
"Such a man is the Antichrist – he denies the Father."
1 John 2:22

• He lies.
"Who is the liar? Such a man is the Antichrist." *1 John 2:22*

• He deceives.
"Many deceivers, who do not acknowledge Jesus Christ as coming in the flesh, have gone out into the world."
2 John 7

The man of lawlessness

The "man of lawlessness," or "wicked one," is mentioned by Paul.

Paul tells us about him:
"Don't let anyone deceive you in any way, for that day will not come until the rebellion occurs and the man of lawlessness is revealed, the man doomed to destruction. He will oppose and will exalt himself over everything that is called God or is worshiped, so that he sets himself up in God's Temple, proclaiming himself to be God."
2 Thessalonians 2:3-4

The man of lawlessness looks like the worst kind of Antichrist. His rebellion against Jesus is horrific. But his final defeat is assured. He is a man "doomed to destruction."
2 Thessalonians 2:3

Satan's work

Describing the foe
The meaning of the name "Satan" is "adversary."

Satan in the Old Testament

Opposition to God
Satan opposes God's servants Job (Job 1:6-12) and David (1 Chronicles 21:1).

In Genesis 3:1 Satan was clearly at work through the serpent in the Garden of Eden.

Satan in the New Testament

Satan's active opposition to Jesus
• Confrontation in the desert. Even before Jesus started his public work as a teacher and healer, Satan launched an assault on him. In Matthew 4:1-11 we see how Satan attacked Jesus over three particular things (see verses 3, 6 and 9).
• Satan tries to undermine Jesus' preaching work. "Some people are like seed along the path, where the word is sown. As soon as they hear it, Satan comes and takes away the word that was sown in them." *Mark 4:15*
In the parable of the weeds, Jesus explains that "the weeds are the sons of the evil one, and the enemy who sows them is the Devil." *Matthew 13:24-30; 36-43; especially verses 37-39*
• Satan attacks Jesus' followers. "Simon, Simon, Satan has asked to sift you as wheat. But I have prayed for you, Simon, that your faith may not fail." *Luke 22:31-32*

Satan uses others against Jesus and his followers
• Judas.
  "Then Satan entered Judas, called Iscariot, one of the Twelve." *Luke 22:3*
• Ananias.
  "Then Peter said, 'Ananias, how is it that Satan has so filled your heart?'" *Acts 5:3*

Satan, a master of disguises

Satan often manages to defeat us because he is a master of the art of deception.

- Sometimes he prowls around as if he has all the strength of a lion.
  "Your enemy the Devil prowls around like a roaring lion looking for someone to devour." *1 Peter 5:8*
- Sometimes he goes around in an angelic disguise.
  "Satan himself masquerades as an angel of light." *2 Corinthians 11:14*
- Sometimes he goes around in the guise of a friend of Jesus.
  "Jesus turned to Peter and said, 'Get behind me, Satan! You are a stumbling-block to me.'" *Matthew 16:23*

A few of Satan's characteristics

Christians are not meant to be ignorant about Satan's devices. Paul once wrote: "We are not unaware of his [Satan's] devices." *2 Corinthians 2:11*

- A deceiver. *Revelation 12:9*
- A liar. *John 8:44*
- A murderer. *John 8:44*

Note on demons

Satan opposed Jesus by using his agents, demons, to possess people.
Jesus showed his divine power when he expelled demons from people. Jesus drove out demons "by the finger [the power and authority] of God." *Luke 11:20*

What will be the end of Satan?

- Satan's days are numbered. Jesus came to destroy him and his evil deeds: "The reason the Son of God appeared was to destroy the Devil's work." *1 John 3:8*
- His final defeat is certain: "The God of peace will soon crush Satan under your feet." *Romans 16:20*

The second coming of Jesus

Concerns about the second coming

Paul's Christian friends at Thessalonica were clearly upset by some of the prophecies about the end of the world. Then, as now, there were numerous false ideas circulating about Jesus' second coming. So Paul wrote to them, saying: "Concerning the coming of our Lord Jesus Christ and our being gathered to him, we ask you, brothers, not to become easily unsettled or alarmed by some prophecy, report or letter supposed to have come from us, saying that the Day of the Lord has already come." *2 Thessalonians 2:1-2*

Comparing the first and second coming of Jesus

First coming	Second coming
Jesus came quietly.	Jesus will come in glory.
Jesus lived in one region of the world.	Jesus will make a global return.
Most people paid no attention to Jesus.	Everyone will acknowledge him.

Talking about the second coming

"At that time men will see the Son of Man coming in clouds with great power and glory." *Mark 13:26*

"For as lightning that comes from the east is visible even in the west, so will be the coming of the Son of Man." *Matthew 24:27*

"He will punish those who do not ... obey the gospel of our Lord Jesus."
2 Thessalonians 1:8

Why do we believe that Jesus will come again?

• Because Jesus promised that he would.
• It is clearly taught throughout the New Testament.
  "For the Lord himself will come down from heaven."
  1 Thessalonians 4:16

"This same Jesus, who has been taken from you into heaven [at the time of the ascension of Jesus], will come back in the same way you have seen him go into heaven." *Acts 1:11*

When Jesus returns

For Christians it will be:
- The moment of final salvation for them.
- They will be with Jesus for ever.
- World order will be recreated.

"For the Lord himself will come down from heaven. ... And so we will be with the Lord for ever."
1 Thessalonians 4:16-17.

Views on the return of Jesus

Here are ideas about Jesus' return from six different writers in the New Testament.

Writer	Key idea	Bible reference
James	Justice	*James 5:1-7*
Paul	Being caught up (with Jesus)	*1 Thessalonians 4:16-17*
Jude	Judgment	*Jude 14-15*
The writer of Hebrews	Jesus' reappearance	*Hebrews 9:28*
John	Purity	*1 John 3:3*
Peter	Jesus' majesty	*2 Peter 1:16*

The resurrection for Christians

Jesus prophesies his own resurrection

Jesus often told his disciples that he had to die in
Jerusalem. But he also predicted his resurrection:
"From that time on Jesus began to explain to his
disciples that he must go to Jerusalem and suffer
many things ... and that he must be killed and on
the third day be raised to life." *Matthew 16:21*

Jesus also predicted a more general resurrection

Jesus' own resurrection was, in many ways, a kind of
prototype of the resurrection promised to Christians. For Jesus
promised that all his followers would also go through a
resurrection: "Do not be amazed at this, for a time is coming
when all who are in their graves will hear his voice and come out
– those who have done good will rise to live, and those who have
done evil will rise to be condemned." *John 5:28-29*

Paul describes resurrection

Paul used a number of analogies to explain what resurrection
will be like for Christians.
- From seed to plant. When we die, it is like a seed being
  planted. In heaven the seed is transformed into a plant.
- From an earthly body to a spiritual body. When Paul talks
  about the resurrection of the "body" for Christians, he is
  talking about our spiritual resurrection: "I declare to you,
  brothers, that flesh and blood cannot inherit the kingdom of
  God, nor does the perishable inherit the imperishable."
  1 Corinthians 15:50

On earth – the burial	In heaven – the harvest
The body is perishable/mortal.	The body is raised, imperishable/immortal.
The body is ugly, sown in dishonor.	The body is beautiful, raised in honor.
The body is weak.	The body is strong and raised in power.
A physical body is buried.	A spiritual body is raised.

New bodies

Paul describes how our earthly bodies are changed in resurrection, in 1 Corinthians 15:51-55.

• We will all be changed (so do not worry if on earth you have a disabled or diseased body).
• The dead will be raised imperishable.
• What is mortal will be changed into what is immortal.
• Death will be destroyed; victory over death will be complete!

Stand firm

The conclusion of Paul's chapter on this subject in 1 Corinthians 15 ends with words of great encouragement: "Therefore, my dear brothers, stand firm. Let nothing move you. Always give yourselves full to the work of the Lord, because you know that your labor in the Lord is not in vain." *1 Corinthians 15:58*

Belief in the resurrection brings hope

Belief in the resurrection of our deceased Christian friends and relatives gives to Christians a hope which others do not have. As Paul says, referring to mourning for Christians who have died, "If only for this life we have hope in Christ, we are to be pitied more than all men." *1 Corinthians 15:19*

John's amazing vision

The Book of Revelation
Chapter 20 of the Book of Revelation contains John's own account of what he saw in his vision of the end of the world.

A great white throne

"Then I saw a great white throne and him who was seated on it. Earth and sky fled from his presence, and there was no place for them."
Revelation 20:11

The interpretation
God was often pictured as ruling and making judgments from his throne in the Old Testament. The idea of God's throne of judgment in heaven is visualized early on in the Book of Revelation: "... and there before me was a throne in heaven with someone sitting on it." *Revelation 4:2*

The dead

"And I saw the dead, great and small, standing before the throne, and books were opened. Another book was opened, which is the book of life. The dead were judged according to what they had done as recorded in the books."
Revelation 20:12

The interpretation
The Bible rules out two things about God's judgment. There is no possibility of reincarnation, and once we are dead there is nothing that anybody else can do to help us. Hebrews 9:27 says, "Just as man is destined to die once, and after that to face judgment..."

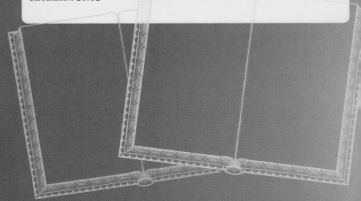

Judgment

"The sea gave up the dead that were in it, and death and Hades gave up the dead that were in them, and each person was judged according to what he had done."
Revelation 20:13

The interpretation

• Judgment "according to what he had done," does not mean that we do not need faith. Good deeds without faith are useless. In fact, in God's sight, good deeds without trust in God are not really good deeds.

• Because of our faith in Jesus, on judgment day God will see the righteousness of Jesus in us, and so we will pass from "death to life." John's Gospel says, "Whoever hears my word and believes him who sent me has eternal life and will not be condemned; he has crossed over from death to life."
John 5:24

The second death

"Then death and Hades were thrown into the lake of fire. The lake of fire is the second death. If anyone's name was not found written in the book of life, he was thrown into the lake of fire."
Revelation 20:14-15

The interpretation

These verses teach that, after we die, we will be judged by God. The "second death" is reserved for those whose names have not been written in the book of life, God's record of everyone who is going to heaven.

There is a wonderful promise in Revelation 3:5 where the Spirit says about faithful followers of Jesus: "I will never blot out his name from the book of life, but will acknowledge his name before my Father and his angels."

What is the "new Jerusalem"?

In the prophetic visions of the Old Testament, the people of Israel are restored to their land in peace and prosperity at the end of history.

Jerusalem is frequently the focal point of such prophecies. Some scholars refer to this as the "new Jerusalem." Other scholars reserve the name "new Jerusalem" for the heavenly, holy city.

DESCRIPTIONS OF THE NEW JERUSALEM

People will worship at Jerusalem
And in that day a great trumpet will sound. Those who are perishing in Assyria and those who are exiled in Egypt will come and worship the Lord on the holy mountain in Jerusalem.
Isaiah 27:13

Jerusalem will be a delight
But be glad and rejoice for ever in what I will create, for I will create Jerusalem to be a delight and its people a joy. *Isaiah 65:18*

It will be a time of safety for Jerusalem
In those days Judah will be saved and Jerusalem will live in safety. This is the name by which it will be called: The Lord Our Righteousness.
Jeremiah 33:16

The vision of the new Jerusalem, the Holy City
In John's vision of the new Jerusalem in the Book of Revelation, the one thing that is missing is the Temple: "I did not see a Temple in the city." *Revelation 21:22*

Then I saw a new heaven and a new earth,
for the first heaven and the first earth had passed away,
and there was no longer any sea.
I saw the Holy City,
the new Jerusalem,
coming down out of heaven from God,
prepared as a bride beautifully dressed for her husband.
And I heard a loud voice from the throne saying,
"Now the dwelling of God is with human beings,
and he will live with them.
They will be his people,
and God himself will be with them and be their God.
He will wipe every tear from their eyes.
There will be no more death
or mourning
or crying
or pain,
for the old order of things has passed away."
He who was seated on the throne said,
"I am making everything new!"
Then he said,
"Write this down,
for these words are trustworthy and true."
Revelation 21:1-5

To think over

The nineteenth-century anti-slave campaigner and social
reformer, William Wilberforce, said he thought about heaven
every day, so he could live a better life on earth.

A study of heaven

What will heaven be like?

The Book of Revelation tells us more about heaven than any other book in the Bible. A good place to start is to read chapters 21 and 22.

God's presence

"Now the dwelling of God is with men [i.e. people], and he will live with them. They will be his people, and God himself will be with them and be their God." *Revelation 21:3*

God's presence is the most attractive thing about heaven. In heaven we will know and experience God more wonderfully than has ever been possible on earth. Our sight of God will be totally unclouded: "They will see his face." *Revelation 22:4*

What is absent in heaven?

- Tears. *Revelation 21:4*
- Death. *Revelation 21:4*
- Mourning. *Revelation 21:4*
- Crying. *Revelation 21:4*
- Pain. *Revelation 21:40*
- The Temple. *Revelation 21:22*
- The sun and the moon. *Revelation 21:23*

In heaven God will not only remove our tears, but remove the causes of our tears: "He will wipe away every tear from their eyes." *Revelation 21:4*

God's presence is so immediate and overwhelming that the Temple is no longer needed in heaven: "I did not see a Temple in [heaven] because the Lord God Almighty and the Lamb are its Temple." *Revelation 21:22*

God's light illuminates heaven: "The city does not need the sun or the moon to shine on it, for the glory of God gives it light, and the Lamb is its lamp." *Revelation 21:23*

Who is allowed into heaven and who is barred?

People who are allowed into heaven

Those who have put their trust in Jesus, who have had their spiritual thirst quenched by the love and forgiveness of Jesus: "To him who is thirsty I will give to drink without cost from the spring of the water of life." *Revelation 21:6*

Those who have had their sins forgiven – "whose names are written in the Lamb's book of life." *Revelation 21:27*

People who are barred from heaven

Those who decide that they do not want to live in God's presence. "Nothing impure will ever enter [heaven], nor will anyone who does what is shameful or deceitful." *Revelation 21:27*

Prophetic visions

Prophecies in the Book of Isaiah

There are at least five prophetic themes in the Book of Isaiah which remain to be fulfilled.

• God's blessing on the nations

On this mountain the Lord Almighty will prepare
a feast of rich food for all peoples,
a banquet of aged wine -
the best of meats and finest of wines.
On this mountain ... he will swallow up death for ever.
The Sovereign Lord will wipe away the tears
from all faces...
Isaiah 25:6-8. Also read: Isaiah 2:1-4; 60:1-12

• The Day of the Lord

Isaiah mentions the time of judgment, the Day of the Lord, forty-five times.
The Lord Almighty has a day in store
for all the proud and lofty,
for all that is exalted
(and they will be humbled).
Isaiah 2:12. Also read: Isaiah 13:9-13; 24:1-23

• God's people will be the center of God's blessing

The sons of your oppressors will come bowing before you;
all who despise you will bow down at your feet. ...
The sun will no more be your light by day,
nor will the brightness of the moon shine on you,
for the Lord will be your everlasting light,
and your God will be your glory.
Your sun will never set again,
and your moon will wane no more;
the Lord will be your everlasting light,
and your days of sorrow will end.
Isaiah 60:14, 19-20. Also read: Isaiah 1:26; 12:6

• God's blessing on the new Israel

He will judge between the nations
and will settle disputes for many peoples.
They will beat their swords into ploughshares
and their spears into pruning hooks.
Nation will not take up sword against nation,
nor will they train for war any more.
Isaiah 2:4. See also: Isaiah 14:1-3; 59:20-21

• God's blessing on all of creation

The wolf will lie down with the lamb,
the leopard will lie down with the goat,
the calf and the lion and the

yearling together;
and a little child will lead them.
The cow will feed with the bear,
their young will lie down together,
and the lion will eat straw like
    the ox.

The infant will play near the hole
    of the cobra,
and the young child put his hand
    into the viper's nest.
Isaiah 11:6-8.
See also: Isaiah 65:17; 66:22

Daniel interprets a dream in a prophetic way

Nebuchadnezzar's dream

You looked, O king, and there before you stood a large statue – an enormous, dazzling statue, awesome in appearance. The head of the statue was made of pure gold, its chest and arms of silver, its belly and thighs of bronze, its legs of iron, its feet partly of iron and partly of baked clay. While you were watching, a rock was cut out, but not by human hands. It struck the statue on its feet of iron and clay and smashed them. Then the iron, the clay, the bronze, the silver and the gold were broken to pieces at the same time and became like chaff on the threshing-floor in the summer. The wind swept them away without leaving a trace. But the rock that struck the statue became a huge mountain and filled the whole earth. *Daniel 2:31-35*

The interpretation Daniel gave Nebuchadnezzar for his dream follows in Daniel 2:36-49. It described four empires, which were Nebuchadnezzar's empire (the Babylonian), and the three empires that followed it (the Medeo-Persian, the Greek and the Roman). Many scholars believe that the rock which became a mountain refers to Christ and the Church.

Seventy weeks

Daniel writes about "seventy sevens" of years, 490 years: "Seventy 'sevens' are decreed for your people and your holy city to finish transgression." *Daniel 9:24*
Details about this period of time are listed in Daniel 9:25-27. Some see predictions of Jesus' death, and the destruction of Jerusalem here.

Something to do

One way of understanding the Book of Daniel is to read it alongside other parts of the Bible.
- With Daniel chapters 7-12 read Mark 13, Matthew 24 and Luke 21.
- With Daniel 9:27 read Revelation 11:1-3.
- With Daniel 9:20-27 read Matthew 24:1-44, 2 Peter 3 and Revelation 11.

Decoding the prophetic lingo

The prophets were versatile if nothing else. They communicated their God-given messages in a variety of expected and unexpected ways.

Parables

The prophets sometimes wrapped up their messages in parables and allegories: see *Isaiah 5:1-7; Ezekiel 16:1-63.*

A parable fit for a king (or, rather, fit for an adulterer and murderer!)

The Lord sent Nathan to David. When he came to him, he said, "There were two men in a certain town, one rich and the other poor. The rich man had a very large number of sheep and cattle, but the poor man had nothing except one little ewe lamb that he had bought. He raised it, and it grew up with him and his children. It shared his food, drank from his cup and even slept in his arms. It was like a daughter to him."

"Now a traveler came to the rich man, but the rich man refrained from making one of his own sheep or cattle to prepare a meal for the traveler who had come to him. Instead, he took the ewe lamb that belonged to the poor man and prepared it for the one who had come to him."

David turned with anger against the man and said to Nathan, "As surely as the Lord lives, the man who did this deserves to die! He must pay for that lamb four times over, because he did such a thing and had no pity."

Then Nathan said to David, "You are the man!"
2 Samuel 12:1-7

Read 2 Samuel 11, which gives the background to the parable.

Symbolic actions: acting out the message

The prophets would go to any lengths to convey their divine messages.

- Elijah told Joash to shoot arrows to represent victories over Syria. *2 Kings 13:15-19*
- Isaiah walked around naked and barefoot. *Isaiah 20*
- Jeremiah bought and hid a linen belt in a crevice in the rocks. *Jeremiah 13*
- Jeremiah smashed up pots in the potter's house. *Jeremiah 19*
- Ahijah tore his new coat into twelve pieces and gave Jeroboam ten of them. *1 Kings 11*
- Ezekiel besieged a model city. *Ezekiel 4*
- Ezekiel dug through the wall of a house. *Ezekiel 12*
- Ezekiel did not mourn for his dead wife. *Ezekiel 24*

Prophecies in the Spirit

These were not very common, but they appear in the Old Testament, and the whole of the Book of Revelation was written while John was "in the Spirit." *Revelation 1:10*

- Moses and the seventy elders experienced prophetic overwhelming by the Spirit. See *Numbers 11:24-30*.
- Saul had an overwhelming experience of God's Spirit in relation to prophecy. *1 Samuel 10:6*

Prophetic visions

- Daniel's visions foretold the future. *Daniel 7-12*
- Ezekiel's vision predicted that God's glory would be withdrawn from the Temple before it was destroyed. *Ezekiel 8-11*
- Zechariah's book has eight visions in it. *Zechariah 1:7-6:8*
- Nearly all the Book of Revelation is a vision.

The teaching of the prophets

We tend to think of the prophets as people who predicted future events and went around scolding everyone in sight! But prophets also had a major role as teachers of God's revelation.

To think over

- The prophets give us many wonderful promises.

  "You will keep in perfect peace him whose mind is steadfast, because he trusts in you." *Isaiah 26:3*

How to read the prophetic signs

It's one thing to read the prophecies in the Bible, but it's quite another thing to understand some of them and to interpret them correctly.

How are the Old Testament prophecies fulfilled?

There are usually three stages in their fulfillment:

- Literal
- Spiritual
- Final

Take the example of the promise to Abraham:

Abraham was promised that he would have countless descendants, at a time when he was childless and his wife was beyond the age to bear children.

"The word of the Lord came to Abraham in a vision: ... 'Look up at the heavens and count the stars – if indeed you can count them.' Then [the Lord] said to [Abraham], 'So shall your offspring be.'"
Genesis 15:1, 5

After Abraham showed that he was prepared to sacrifice his only son Isaac, the Lord said:

"I will surely bless you and make your descendants as numerous as the stars in the sky and as the sand on the seashore." *Genesis 22:17*

Stage one: literal

The promise to Abraham was fulfilled in the birth of Isaac. The Israelites (the Jews of the New Testament) are descended from Abraham, and Isaac.

In King Solomon's day, the "people of Judah and Israel were as numerous as the sand on the seashore." *1 Kings 4:20*

Stage two: spiritual

The promise is fulfilled today in a spiritual way. Jesus once explained that to be "Abraham's children" people needed to behave as Abraham did. *See John 8:39-41.* Christians today are Abraham's spiritual heirs.

> "Those who believe are children of Abraham." *Galatians 3:7*

Stage three: final

The original promise made to Abraham will only be fully and finally completed in heaven. Abraham's countless "children" are described in the book of Revelation:

> "After this I looked and there before me was a great multitude that no one could count, from every nation, tribe, people and language, standing before the throne and in front of the Lamb."
> *Revelation 7:9*

Take the example of the rebuilding of the Temple:

• The first stage of fulfillment

The Old Testament prophets predicted that the broken-down Temple would be rebuilt. This happened literally after the Israelites' return from exile. *(See Ezra chapter three)*

• The second stage of fulfillment

Today this prophecy is fulfilled in a spiritual way, since God's Spirit lives in Christians. Paul reminds the Christians who lived in Corinth,

> "Don't you know that you yourselves are God's Temple and that God's Spirit lives in you?" *1 Corinthians 3:16*

The prophecy is also fulfilled in an individual Christian's body:

> "Do you not know that your body is a Temple of the Holy Spirit, who is in you, whom you have received from God?" *1 Corinthians 6:19*

• The third stage of fulfillment

In the heavenly Jerusalem, this prophecy about the rebuilding of the Temple is completely fulfilled. There will not even be a Temple there:

> "I did not see a Temple in the city, because the Lord God Almighty and the Lamb are its Temple." *Revelation 21:22*

Unravel the secret Biblical symbols

Symbols and signs

"The Lord himself will give you a sign," wrote the prophet Isaiah.

The sign was a strange one. A virgin would give birth to a son: see Isaiah 7:14. Matthew interprets this as a prophecy about Jesus: see Matthew 1:23.

Old Testament prediction	Messianic theme	New Testament fulfillment
"But you, Bethlehem Ephrathah, though you are small among the clans of Judah, out of you will come for me one who will be ruler over Israel." *Micah 5:2*	**The Messiah's place of birth**	"So Joseph also went up from the town of Nazareth in Galilee to Judea, to Bethlehem the town of David. ... While they were there ... [Mary] gave birth to her firstborn, a son." *Luke 2:4, 6-7*
"Therefore the Lord himself will give you a sign: the virgin will be with child and will give birth to a son." *Isaiah 7:14*	**A virgin will give birth to a son**	"In the sixth month, God sent the angel Gabriel to Nazareth ... to a virgin. ... The virgin's name was Mary." *Luke 1:26-27*
"The virgin will be with child and will give birth to a son, and will call him Immanuel." *Isaiah 7:14*	**The name of the Messiah**	"The virgin will be with child and will give birth to a son, and they will call him Immanuel – which means, 'God with us.' " *Matthew 1:23*

In the prophecies of the Old Testament there are many other seemingly unconnected things – places and people which are symbols of God's promised Messiah. "Bethlehem," a "virgin," a "messenger," a "king," a "prophet," the "year of the Lord's favor" (see Isaiah 61:1-3), and a "king riding into Jerusalem on a donkey," are linked to each other in this way.

To think over
• From his actions in the four gospels, think of the ways in which Jesus fulfilled the prophecy of Isaiah 61:1-3.

Old Testament prediction	Messianic theme	New Testament fulfillment
"See, I will send my messenger, who will prepare the way before me." *Malachi 3:1*	**John the Baptist was the messenger**	[Jesus said about John the Baptist,] "This is the one about whom it is written: 'I will send my messenger ahead of you, who will prepare your way before you.'" *Luke 7:27*
"The Lord will raise up for you a prophet like me from among your own brothers. You must listen to him." *Deuteronomy 18:15*	**Jesus is seen as the predicted prophet**	[Peter said:] "For Moses said, 'The Lord your God will raise up for you a prophet like me from among your own people; you must listen to everything he tells you.'" *Acts 3:22*
"Rejoice greatly, O Daughter of Zion! Shout, Daughter of Jerusalem! See, your king comes to you, righteous and having salvation, gentle and riding on a donkey." *Zechariah 9:9*	**The Messiah would enter Jerusalem riding a donkey**	"When they brought the colt to Jesus and threw their cloaks over it, he sat on it. Many people spread their cloaks on the road, while others spread branches they had cut in the fields. ... Jesus entered Jerusalem." *Mark 11:7-8, 11*

Prophecy as forth-telling, not just foretelling

We tend to think that the main work of prophets was to predict the future. Their work was also "forth-telling" as well as "foretelling" the future. "Forth-telling" was passing on to people God's message for them at that time.

The importance of Old Testament prophets in the life of the nation

Prophets advised and corrected kings and queens, as well as political and religious leaders.

Prophet	Incident	Bible reference
Nathan	Rebukes David for adultery and murder. David repents.	2 Samuel 12
Unnamed prophet	Opposes Jeroboam I for supporting pagan religion in Israel.	1 Kings 13
Elijah	Has a showdown with the prophets of Baal on Mount Carmel.	1 Kings 18
Unnamed prophet	Helps Ahab's army defeat Syria.	1 Kings 20
Elijah	Condemns Ahab for murdering Naboth and for taking his vineyard.	1 Kings 21
Elisha	Predicts that the siege of Samaria will be lifted.	2 Kings 7

Famine in besieged Samaria

Ben-Hadad king of Aram mobilized his entire army and marched up and laid siege to Samaria. There was a great famine in the city; the siege lasted so long that a donkey's head was sold for eighty shekels of silver....

Elisha said, "Hear the word of the Lord. This is what the Lord says: about this time tomorrow, a measure of flour or two measures of barley will sell for a shekel at the gates of Samaria."

The officer on whose arm the king was leaning said to the man of God, "Look, even if the Lord should open the floodgates of the heavens, could this happen?"

Prophet	Incident	Bible reference
Elisha	Sends a prophet to anoint General Jehu to be Israel's king.	2 Kings 9
Isaiah	Predicts that the Assyrian army will retreat.	2 Kings 19
Hanani	Tells off King Asa and is imprisoned as a result.	2 Chronicles 16
Micaiah	Predicts that Ahab will be killed in battle.	2 Chronicles 18
Jeremiah	Is imprisoned for predicting the fall of Jerusalem and advising surrender to the Babylonians.	Jeremiah 37-38
Daniel	Interprets King Nebuchadnezzar's dream and warns him of the approaching seven years of insanity.	Daniel 2, 4
Amos	In the market town of Bethel, he speaks out against the oppression and corruption of religious and social leaders.	Amos 7

Kindness to the underprivileged

As well as advising kings and rulers, prophets had time for ordinary people. Read Elijah's message for two widows, in 1 Kings 17 and 2 Kings 4:1-7.

... At dusk [four lepers from Samaria] got up and went to the camp of the Arameans. When they reached the edge of the camp not a man was there, for the Lord had caused the Arameans to hear the sound of chariots and horses and a great army ... so they got up and fled in the dusk and abandoned their tents.

... Then the people [of Samaria] went out and plundered the camp of the Arameans. So a measure of flour sold for a shekel and two measures of barley sold for a shekel, as the Lord had said.
2 Kings 6:24-7:16

How Jesus said he was fulfilling the prophets

As well as fulfilling the Old Testament prophecies about the Messiah, Jesus himself was the greatest prophet of all time.

Jesus is recognized as a prophet and teacher from God

• "The crowds answered, 'This is Jesus, the prophet from Nazareth in Galilee.'" *Matthew 21:11*
• After the son of the widow of Nain had been raised to life: "They were filled with awe and praised God. 'A great prophet has appeared among us,' they said. 'God has come to help his people.'" *Luke 7:16*

Jesus is seen to have the same characteristics as Old Testament prophets

• "Rabbi, we know you are a teacher who has come from God. For no one could perform the miraculous signs you are doing if God were not with him." *John 3:2*

Jesus uses the titles "prophet" and "teacher" of himself

• "But Jesus said to them, 'Only in his home town and in his own house is a prophet without honor.'" *Matthew 13:57*
• "In any case, I must keep going today and tomorrow and the next day – for surely no prophet can die outside Jerusalem!" *Luke 13:33*
• "You call me 'Teacher' and 'Lord', and rightly so, for that is what I am. Now that I, your Lord and Teacher, have washed your feet, you also should wash one another's feet. I have set you an example that you should do as I have done for you. I tell you the truth, no servant is greater than his master, nor is a messenger greater than the one who sent him. Now that you know these things, you will be blessed if you do them." *John 13:13-17*

Jesus is seen to be the ultimate fulfillment of the prophecies of Abraham and Moses

• **The fulfillment of Abraham's prophecy.**

"Indeed, all the prophets from Samuel on, as many as have spoken, have foretold these days. And you are heirs of the prophets and of the covenant God made with your fathers. He said to Abraham, 'Through your offspring all peoples on earth will be blessed.' When God raised up his servant, he sent him first to you to bless you by turning each of you from your wicked ways." *Acts 3:24-26*

• **The fulfillment of Moses' prophecy.**

"This is that Moses who told the Israelites, 'God will send you a prophet like me from your own people.'" *Acts 7:37*

Jesus sends the prophets

• "Therefore I am sending you prophets and wise men and teachers. Some of them you will kill and crucify; others you will flog in your synagogues and pursue from town to town. ..."

"O Jerusalem, Jerusalem, you who kill the prophets and stone those sent to you, how often I have longed to gather your children together, as a hen gathers her chicks under her wings, but you were not willing."
Matthew 23:34, 37

Jesus not only speaks the words of God, he is the Word of God

• "His name is the Word of God." *Revelation 19:13*
• "In the beginning was the Word, and the Word was with God, and the Word was God. He was with God in the beginning." *John 1:1*

Jesus' arrest fulfills the scriptures

• "'Am I leading a rebellion,' said Jesus, 'that you have come out with swords and clubs to capture me? Every day I was with you, teaching in the Temple courts, and you did not arrest me. But the scriptures must be fulfilled.'" *Mark 14:48-49*

To think over

• There is one way to be "greater" than the great Old Testament prophet Elijah, according to the greatest prophet of all time, Jesus: "I tell you the truth: among those born of women there has not risen anyone greater than John the Baptist; yet he who is least in the kingdom of heaven is greater than he."
Matthew 11:11

Why Matthew makes 65 references to the Old Testament

Matthew's Gospel presents Jesus as Israel's promised Messiah. Matthew, a Jew, tells his countrymen that Jesus is the King of the Jews, the long-awaited Messiah. The Jewish readers would have known all the references Matthew makes to the Old Testament. Matthew is showing that all the prophecies and quotations point to Jesus.

Matthew	Theme	Old Testament
1:3-6	Genealogy of Jesus	Ruth 4:18-22
1:7-11	Genealogy of Jesus	1 Chronicles 3:10-17
1:23	Virgin with child	Isaiah 7:14
2:6	Bethlehem	Micah 5:2
2:15	Out of Egypt I called my son	Hosea 11:1
2:18	Weeping in Ramah	Jeremiah 31:15
3:3	Prepare the way for the Lord	Isaiah 40:3
3:17	This is my Son	Psalm 2:7, Isaiah 42:1
4:4	Man shall not live by bread alone	Deuteronomy 8:3
4:6	God's protective angels	Psalm 91:11-12
4:7	Do not put God to the test	Deuteronomy 6:16
4:10	Worship God	Deuteronomy 6:13
4:16	A light has dawned	Isaiah 9:1-2
5:21	Do not murder	Exodus 20:13
5:27	Do not commit adultery	Exodus 20:14
5:31	A certificate of divorce	Deuteronomy 24:1-4
5:38	An eye for an eye	Exodus 21:24, Leviticus 24:20 Deuteronomy 19:21
5:43	Love your enemy	Leviticus 19:18
8:17	He carried our diseases	Isaiah 53:4
9:13	I desire mercy, not sacrifice	Hosea 6:6
10:35-36	A man against his father	Micah 7:6
11:10	I will send my messenger	Malachi 3:1
12:7	I desire mercy, not sacrifice	Hosea 6:6
12:18-21	I will put my Spirit on him	Isaiah 42:1-4
12:42	Queen of the South	1 Kings 10:1
13:14-15	Hearing without understanding	Isaiah 6:9-10
13:35	Speaking in parables	Psalm 78:2
15:4	Honor your parents	Exodus 20:12, Deuteronomy 5:16

Matthew constantly speaks about the Old Testament being fulfilled. He says that the events of the New Testament that focused on Jesus fulfilled Old Testament prophecies. He specifically states this truth twelve times in his gospel: "All this took place to fulfill what the Lord had said through the prophet..." (Matthew 1:22.) See also Matthew 2:15, 23; 3:15; 4:14; 5:17; 8:17; 12:17; 13:14, 35; 21:4; 27:9.

Something to do
• Look up the Old Testament references to see how they show that Jesus is the Messiah.

Matthew	Theme	Old Testament
15:4	Cursing your parents	Exodus 21:17, Leviticus 20:9
15:8-9	Hearts far from God	Isaiah 29:13
18:16	Two or three witnesses	Deuteronomy 19:15
19:4	Leaving parents	Genesis 1:27
19:5	Becoming one flesh	Genesis 2:24
19:19	Honor your parents	Exodus 20:12-16, Deuteronomy 5:16-20
19:19	Love your neighbor	Leviticus 19:18
21:5	Riding on a donkey	Zechariah 9:9
21:9	Blessed is he who comes in the name of the Lord	Psalm 118:26
21:13	A house of prayer	Isaiah 56:7
21:13	A den of robbers	Jeremiah 7:11
21:16	From the lips of children	Psalm 8:2
21:42	The capstone	Psalm 118:22-23
22:32	I am the God of Abraham	Exodus 3:6
22:37	Love God	Deuteronomy 6:5
22:39	Love your neighbor	Leviticus 19:18
22:44	Sit at my right hand	Psalm 110:1
23:39	Blessed is he who comes ...	Psalm 118:26
24:15	The abomination	Daniel 9:27, Daniel 11:31, Daniel 12:11
24:29	The sun will be darkened	Isaiah 13:10, Isaiah 34:4
26:24	The Suffering Servant	Isaiah 53
26:30	Psalms sung at the Passover	Psalms 115-118
26:31	I will strike the shepherd	Zechariah 13:7
26:54	Scriptures fulfilled	Zechariah 13:7
27:10	Buy the potter's field	Zechariah 11:12-13, Jeremiah 19:1-13, Jeremiah 32:6-9
27:46	Eloi, Eloi, lama sabachthani?	Psalm 22:1

Jesus in the Psalms

Jesus can be seen very clearly in many of the psalms, but none more so than Psalms 22, 23 and 24.

PSALM 22	PSALM 23	PSALM 24
Savior	Shepherd	Sovereign
Sword	Staff	Scepter
Suffering	Supply/provision	Splendour
The cross	The crook	The crown
Gloom	Goodness	Greatness
Grace	Guidance	Glory
Pardon	Peace	Power
Wrath	Walk/journey	Welcome
Cry for help	Comfort	Conquest
Misery	Mercy	Majesty
Rejection	Refreshment	Reign
He dies	He lives	He is coming

Something to do
- Read through Psalms 22, 23 and 24, noting the verses in which the words, concepts and descriptions in the above lists come. Then link them to incidents in the life of Jesus.
- For example, the first word listed under Psalm 22 is "savior." This theme is found in verse 5 of Psalm 22, "They cried to you and were saved."
- Matthew 1:21 is one of the many New Testament references to Jesus as savior: "You are to give him the name Jesus, because he will save his people from their sins."

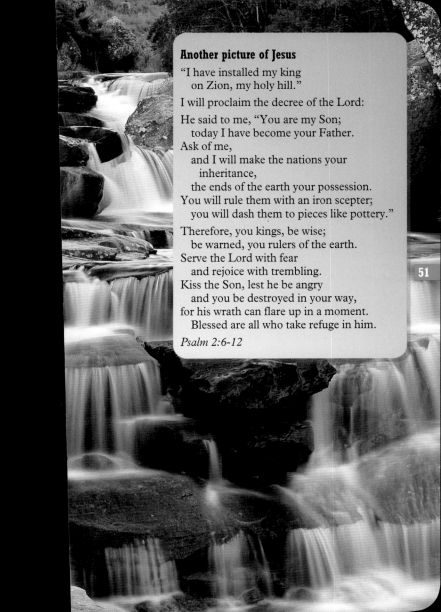

Another picture of Jesus

"I have installed my king
 on Zion, my holy hill."

I will proclaim the decree of the Lord:

He said to me, "You are my Son;
 today I have become your Father.
Ask of me,
 and I will make the nations your
 inheritance,
 the ends of the earth your possession.
You will rule them with an iron scepter;
 you will dash them to pieces like pottery."

Therefore, you kings, be wise;
 be warned, you rulers of the earth.
Serve the Lord with fear
 and rejoice with trembling.
Kiss the Son, lest he be angry
 and you be destroyed in your way,
for his wrath can flare up in a moment.
 Blessed are all who take refuge in him.

Psalm 2:6-12

51

Prophecies in Isaiah about Jesus' death

Isaiah 53 tells us more about Jesus' death than any other chapter in the Old Testament.

Predictions in Isaiah 53	Theme	Fulfilled by Jesus
"Raised and lifted up and highly exalted." *Isaiah 52:13*	**Jesus' exaltation**	"Therefore God highly exalted him to the highest place." *Philippians 2:9*
"He was despised and rejected by men." *Isaiah 53:3*	**Jesus was despised**	"The people stood watching, and the rulers sneered at him." *Luke 23:35*
"He took up our infirmities and carried our sorrows." *Isaiah 53:4*	**Jesus' work of healing**	"This was to fulfill what was spoken through the prophet Isaiah: 'He took up our infirmities and carried our diseases.' " *Matthew 8:17*
"He was pierced for our transgressions." *Isaiah 53:5*	**Jesus was pierced**	"One of the soldiers pierced Jesus' side with a spear, bringing a sudden flow of blood and water." *John 19:34*
"The Lord has laid on him the iniquity of us all." *Isaiah 53:6*	**Jesus took our sin**	"He himself bore our sins in his body on the tree [cross]." *1 Peter 2:24*
"He was oppressed and afflicted, yet he did not open his mouth; ... he had done no violence, nor was any deceit in his mouth." *Isaiah 53:7, 9*	**Jesus' example of suffering**	"Christ suffered for you, leaving you an example, that you should follow in his steps. 'He commited no sin, and no deceit was found in his mouth.' When they hurled their insults at him, he did not retaliate." *1 Peter 2:21-23*

Old Testament prediction	Theme	Fulfilled by Jesus' death
"He was assigned a grave with the wicked." *Isaiah 53:9*	**Jesus died with evil people**	"The robbers who were crucified with [Jesus] also heaped insults on him." *Matthew 27:44*
"He will see the light of life." *Isaiah 53:11*	**Jesus' resurrection**	"Christ ... was raised on the third day according to the scriptures." *1 Corinthians 15:3-4*
"He ... was numbered with the transgressors." *Isaiah 53:12*	**Jesus himself claimed to fulfill this prophecy**	"It is written: 'And he was numbered with the transgressors'; and I tell you that this must be fulfilled in me. Yes, what is written about me is reaching its fulfillment." *Luke 22:37*
"For he bore the sins of many." *Isaiah 53:12*	**Jesus bore our sins**	"Christ was sacrificed once to take away the sins of many people." *Hebrews 9:28*
"He ... made intercession for the transgressors." *Isaiah 53:12*	**Jesus prayed for those who nailed him to the cross**	"Jesus said, 'Father, forgive them, for they do not know what they are doing.' " *Luke 23:34*

53

Something to do
• Read through Isaiah 52:13-53:12 to see what other links with Jesus come to your mind.

Eleven links between John and Isaiah

A number of the books of the Bible fit together when they are compared. John's Gospel and the Book of Isaiah are well worth looking at in this way.

Prophetic hints in Isaiah	Themes	Fulfillment in John's Gospel
"He tends his flock like a shepherd: he gathers the lambs in his arms and carries them close to his heart; he gently leads those that have young." *Isaiah 40:11*	**The shepherd and the sheep**	"I am the good shepherd. The good shepherd lays down his life for the sheep. ... I know my sheep and my sheep know me." *John 10:11, 14. See John 10:1-21*
"They will neither hunger nor thirst." *Isaiah 49:10*	**Food for the hungry**	"I am the bread of life. Whoever comes to me will never go hungry." *John 6:35*
"Come, all you who are thirsty, come to the waters; and you who have no money, come, buy and eat! Come, buy wine and milk without money and without cost." *Isaiah 55:1*	**Water for the thirsty**	"On the last great day of the Feast, Jesus stood and said in a loud voice, 'Let anyone who is thirsty come to me and drink.' " *John 7:37*
" 'As for me, this is my covenant with them,' says the Lord. 'My Spirit, who is on you, ... will not depart from [you].' " *Isaiah 59:21*	**The gift of the Holy Spirit**	"But the Counselor, the Holy Spirit, whom the Father will send in my name, will teach you all things and will remind you of everything that I have said to you." *John 14:26*
"I am the Lord your God, who teaches you what is best for you, who directs you in the way you should go." *Isaiah 48:17*	**Divine guidance**	"But when he, the Spirit of truth, comes, he will guide you into all truth." *John 16:13*

"Turn to me and be saved, all you ends of the earth; for I am God, and there is no other." *Isaiah 45:22*	**Salvation for the world**	"I have other sheep that are not of this sheep pen. I must bring them also. They too will listen to my voice, and there shall be one flock and one shepherd." *John 10:16*
"So do not fear, for I am with you; do not be dismayed, for I am your God. I will strengthen you and help you; I will uphold you with my righteous right hand." *Isaiah 41:10*	**Freedom from the grip of fear**	"Do not let your hearts be troubled. Trust in God; trust also in me." *John 14:1*
"He has sent me...to proclaim freedom for the captives." *Isaiah 61:1*	**Spiritual freedom**	"So if the Son sets you free, you will be free indeed." *John 8:36*
"The Sovereign Lord has given me an instructed tongue." *Isaiah 50:4*	**Teaching from God**	"The words that I say to you are not just my own." *John 14:10*
"Then will the eyes of the blind be opened and the ears of the deaf unstopped." *Isaiah 35:5*	**Sight for the blind**	"Jesus said, 'For judgment I have come into this world, so that the blind will see and those who see will become blind.' " *John 9:39*
"I, even I, am he who comforts you." *Isaiah 51:12*	**God who comforts**	"He will give you another Counselor [comforter] to be with you for ever." *John 14:16*

Something to do
• Make a list of other topics you find both in Isaiah and John.

Marks of a genuine prophet

It is not always easy to tell genuine and false prophets apart.

Marks of a false prophet

- A false prophet supports the worship of gods. *Deuteronomy 13:1-5*
- A false prophet denies that Jesus is the Son of God. *1 John 4:1-3*
- A false prophet may be morally suspect: arrogant /corrupt sexually /a lover of money. *2 Peter 2:10-12; Jude 3, 4, 8, 11-13, 16, 19*
- A false prophet's ministry may be full of empty talk. *2 Peter 2:18-19*

Marks of a genuine prophet

- A genuine prophet will speak in the name of the Lord. *Deuteronomy 18:19-20; Jeremiah 28*
- A genuine prophet prophesies accurately. *Deuteronomy 18:22*
- Genuine prophets speak out against injustice.

"You trample on the poor and force him to give you grain…. Seek good, not evil, that you may live. Then the Lord God almighty will be with you, just as he says he is. Hate evil, love good; maintain justice in the courts." *Amos 5:11, 14-15*

Ezekiel's shepherds

God's prophets were sometimes likened to shepherds. The following references are all taken from Ezekiel chapter 34.

Bad shepherds – the false prophets	Good shepherds – the genuine prophets
• They feed themselves, not the flock. *Verses 2-3*	• They give the flock rest in good pastures. *Verse 15*
• They do not take care of the weak and sick. *Verse 4*	• They heal the sick. *Verse 16*
• They do not go and look for the lost. *Verse 4*	• They search out the lost sheep. *Verse 11*
• They do not allow themselves to be fed by the Great Shepherd. *Verse 10*	• They shepherd the flock with justice. *Verse 16*

"Watch out for false prophets. They come to you in sheep's clothing, but inwardly they are ferocious wolves. By their fruits you will recognize them. Do people pick grapes from thorn-bushes, or figs from thistles?" *Matthew 7:15-16*

Testing the spirits

People who claim to be prophets today must be tested by biblical criteria.

"Dear friends, do not believe every spirit, but test the spirits to see whether they are from God, because many false prophets have gone out into the world. This is how you can recognize the Spirit of God: every spirit that acknowledges that Jesus Christ has come in the flesh is from God, but every spirit that does not acknowledge Jesus is not from God." *1 John 4:1-3*

To think over

• "Not everyone who speaks in a spirit is a prophet. The only person who is a prophet is the one who walks in the ways of the Lord." *Didache*

See also: *Are there any genuine prophets today?*, page 64.

Ten prophecies about Jesus and the Holy Spirit

Eight prophecies about Jesus' death

Fulfilled prophecies are seen clearly in the Old Testament predictions which have been fulfilled by the death of Jesus.

Old Testament prediction	Theme	Fulfilled by Jesus' death
"All who see me mock me; they hurl insults, shaking their heads: 'He trusts in the Lord; let the Lord rescue him. Let him deliver him, since he delights in him.' " *Psalm 22:7-8*	**Mocking and insults**	"The people stood watching, and the rulers even sneered at him. They said, 'He saved others; let him save himself if he is the Christ of God, the Chosen One.' " *Luke 23:35*
"They put gall in my food and gave me vinegar for my thirst." *Psalm 69:21*	**Vinegar and gall**	"There they offered Jesus wine to drink, mixed with gall." *Matthew 27:34*
"In return for my friendship they accuse me, but I am a man of prayer." *Psalm 109:4*	**Hostility is met by prayer**	"Father, forgive them, for they do not know what they are doing." *Luke 23:34*
"My God, my God, why have you forsaken me? Why are you so far from saving me, so far from the words of my groaning?" *Psalm 22:1*	**Jesus' words on the cross (1)**	"About the ninth hour Jesus cried out in a loud voice, ... 'My God, my God, why have you forsaken me?' " *Matthew 27:46*
"Into your hands I commit my spirit; redeem me, O Lord, the God of truth." *Psalm 31:5*	**Jesus' words on the cross (2)**	"Jesus called out with a loud voice, 'Father, into your hands I commit my spirit.' " *Luke 23:46*
"They divide my garments among them and cast lots for my clothing." *Psalm 22:18*	**Casting lots for clothing**	"When they had crucified him, they divided up his clothes by casting lots." *Matthew 27:35*
"He protects all his bones, not one of them will be broken." *Psalm 34:20*	**No bones to be broken**	"When they came to Jesus and found that he was already dead, they did not break his legs." *John 19:33*

Old Testament prediction	Theme	Fulfilled by Jesus' death
"They will look on me, the one they have pierced, and they will mourn for him as one mourns for an only child." *Zechariah 12:10*	**The body is pierced**	"One of the soldiers pierced Jesus' side with a spear, bringing a sudden flow of blood and water." *John 19:34*

Two prophecies about the Holy Spirit

Some of the most striking examples of Old Testament prophecies being fulfilled in the New Testament concern the Holy Spirit.

• Joel's prophecy ...
And afterwards,
I will pour out my Spirit on all people.
Your sons and daughters will prophesy,
your old men will dream dreams,
your young men will see visions.
Even on my servants, both men and
    women,
I will pour out my Spirit in those days.
I will show wonders in the heavens
and on the earth,
blood and fire and billows of smoke.
The sun will be turned to darkness
and the moon to blood
before the coming of the great and
    dreadful Day of the Lord.
And everyone who calls
on the name of the Lord will be saved;
for on Mount Zion and in Jerusalem
there will be deliverance,
as the Lord has said,
among the survivors
whom the Lord calls.
Joel 2:28-32

... fulfilled on the Day of Pentecost
When Christians were filled with the Holy Spirit, in Acts 2:1-13, some people said they were drunk! Peter then explained what had happened: "Let me explain this to you. ... These men are not drunk, as you suppose. ... No, this is what was spoken by the prophet Joel." *Acts 2:14-16*

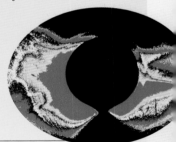

• Ezekiel's prophecy ...
"I will give you a new heart and put a new spirit in you; I will remove from you your heart of stone and give you a heart of flesh. And I will put my Spirit in you and move you to follow my decrees." *Ezekiel 36:26-27*

... fulfilled in every Christian
"You show that you are a letter from Christ ... written not with ink but with the Spirit of the living God." *2 Corinthians 3:3*

A Who's Who? of Bible prophets

The Old Testament prophets

There are 17 books in the Old Testament which are books of the prophets.

Major and minor prophets

The first four books of the prophets, sometimes called the "major" prophets, are Isaiah, Jeremiah, Ezekiel and Daniel. 12 books are sometimes called the "minor" prophets, not because they are unimportant, but because they are much shorter than the first four.

The Book of Lamentations, linked to the Book of Jeremiah, brings the number of prophetic books to 17.

Major prophets

ISAIAH

Isaiah warns about God's judgment against Judah. Salvation will come from the Lord. The word "salvation" is used twenty-six times in Isaiah, but only seven times in all the other prophets' books combined.

Key verse *Isaiah 9:6-7*
Bible link *2 Kings 15:1-20:21; 2 Chronicles 26:16–32:33*

JEREMIAH

Jeremiah warns the people of Judah that Jerusalem will be captured. He prophesies that they will go back to Jerusalem seventy years later.

Key verse *Jeremiah 7:23-24*
Bible link *2 Chronicles 35:25; 36:12; Ezra 1:1; Daniel 9:2*

Minor prophets

HOSEA

Hosea's unfaithful wife is used to illustrate Israel's unfaithfulness to God. Yet God still loves his people and will restore them.

Key verse *Hosea 11:7.* See also *Hosea 14:4.*
Bible link *2 Kings 14:23-18:12*

JOEL

Joel announces that destruction is in store for the wicked. But God's Spirit will be poured out on those who are faithful to God.

Key verse *Joel 2:28*
Bible link *2 Kings 12:1-21*

AMOS

Amos condemns Israel for immorality, corruption, abuse of the legal system and oppression of the poor.

Key verse *Amos 5:24*
Bible link *2 Kings 14:23–15:7*

OBADIAH

Obadiah prophesies Edom's destruction and God's victory.

Key verse *Obadiah 10*
Bible link *2 Chronicles 21:1-20*

JONAH

Jonah preaches against the wicked city of Nineveh.

Key verse *Jonah 4:11*
Bible link *2 Kings 13:10-25*

EZEKIEL

Ezekiel was among the prisoners taken to Babylon. In exile he gives messages of hope about the future.
Key verse *Ezekiel 36:33*
2 Kings 24:8-25:30; 2 Chronicles 36:9-21

DANIEL

Daniel foretells the overthrow of the Gentile world powers and the future deliverance of God's people.
Key verse *Daniel 2:21-22*
Bible link *Ezekiel 14:14, 20; 28:3*

Something to do

• By looking up the references under "Links in the Bible" you will discover the context and background to each Old Testament prophetic book.

Key chapters from the major prophets

Isaiah	Jeremiah	Ezekiel	Daniel
6	1	1	1
40	7	34	2
53	18	37	7

MICAH

Micah warns that Judah will be judged for her injustice.
Key verse *Micah 7:18*
Bible link *2 Chronicles 27:1-32:23*

NAHUM

Nahum prophesies the destruction of Nineveh.
Key verse *Nahum 3:7*
Bible link *2 Chronicles 33:1-20*

HABAKKUK

Habakkuk warns that the ruthless Chaldeans will bring God's judgment on Judah.
Key verse *Habakkuk 2:4*
Bible link *2 Kings 23:31–24:7*

ZEPHANIAH

Zephaniah states that the whole world will be judged, but that restoration is also promised.
Key verse *Zephaniah 2:3*
Bible link *2 Chronicles 34:1-7*

HAGGAI

Haggai scolds the returned exiles for looking after their own prosperity and neglecting God's Temple.
Key verse *Haggai 1:8*
Bible link *Ezra 5:1–6:15*

ZECHARIAH

Zechariah advises the people to repent and rebuild the Temple, because the King will return and reign.
Key verse *Zechariah 9:9*
Bible link *Ezra 5:1–6:15*

MALACHI

Malachi warns that God will punish Judah's spiritual indifference on the coming Day of the Lord.
Key verse *Malachi 3:1*
Bible link *Nehemiah 13:1-31*

What about Bible prophetesses?

There were prophetesses as well as prophets in both the Old Testament and the New Testament.

Old Testament prophetesses	
Name	**Key reference**
Miriam	*Exodus 15:20*
Deborah	*Judges 4:4*
Huldah	*2 Kings 22:14*
Isaiah's unnamed wife	*Isaiah 8:3*

Miriam

Miriam, sister of Moses, led a choral dance to celebrate Israel's deliverance from Egypt.

A prophetess who led the singing

When Pharaoh's horses, chariots and horsemen went into the sea, the Lord brought the waters of the sea back over them, but the Israelites walked through the sea on dry ground. Then Miriam the prophetess, Aaron's sister, took a tambourine in her hand, and all the women followed her, with tambourines and dancing. Miriam sang to them:

"I will sing to the Lord,
  for he is highly exalted.
The horse and its rider
  he has hurled into the sea."
Exodus 15:1

Miriam opposes Moses

From the following incident, we learn about the three ways in which God communicated with his prophets:

- Through visions
- Through dreams
- Through direct revelation

Miriam and Aaron began to talk against Moses ...
"Has the Lord spoken only through Moses?" they asked.
"Listen to my words:
When a prophet of the Lord is among you,
I reveal myself to him in visions,
I speak to him in dreams,
But this is not true of my servant Moses;
he is faithful in all my house.
With him I speak face to face."
Numbers 12:2, 6-8

New Testament prophetesses

Name	Key reference
Mary	*Luke 1:46-55*
Anna	*Luke 2:36*
Philip's four daughters	*Acts 21:9*

Anna

On seeing the infant Jesus presented in the Temple, Anna praises God for the fulfillment of the divine promises.

There was also a prophetess, Anna, the daughter of Phanuel, of the tribe of Asher. She was very old; she had lived with her husband seven years after her marriage, and then was a widow until she was eighty-four. She never left the Temple but worshiped night and day, fasting and praying. Coming up to [Jesus, Mary and Joseph] at that very moment, she gave thanks to God and spoke about the child to all who were looking forward to the redemption of Jerusalem.
Luke 2:36-38

To think over

• There were false prophetesses as well as false prophets in Israel: "Set your face against the daughters of your people who prophesy out of their own imagination." *Ezekiel 13:17*

Are there any genuine prophets today?

Prophecy in the New Testament

Prophets and prophecy did not die out with the Old Testament. Prophecy is a major theme in the New Testament.

Who are the prophets and prophetesses in the New Testament?

A number of people in the New Testament gave voice to prophecies at certain crucial times.

- Zechariah
- Mary
- Anna
- Simeon
- John the Baptist
- The apostle Paul
- Agabus
- Philip's four daughters
- The apostle John – the writer of the Book of Revelation

Prophecy in the Church

Church prophets

These were the people who contributed to the worship of their local churches.
They did this by:
- Proclaiming God's message
- Exhorting
- Encouraging
- Bringing secret sins to light

Paul's teaching about prophecy

Prophecy as a spiritual gift

"Now to each one the manifestation of the Spirit is given for the common good ... to another prophecy." *1 Corinthians 12:1, 10*

Prophecy is singled out

"Follow the way of love and eagerly desire spiritual gifts, especially the gift of prophecy." *1 Corinthians 14:1*

Prophecy today?

Paul wrote: "Are all apostles? Are all prophets? Are all teachers? Do all work miracles?"
1 Corinthians 12:29.
"We have different gifts, according to the grace given to us. If a man's gift is prophesying, let him use it in proportion to his faith." *Romans 12:6*

- Some people believe that Paul's words apply only to the age of the Acts of the Apostles, before the completion of the New Testament. With the writing of the New Testament, it is said, prophets are no longer needed.
- Others believe that Paul's words apply to the whole period between Pentecost and Jesus' second coming. They say that Paul gave no indication that these particular words were temporary.
- One thing is for certain, God uses certain gifted people today to "forth-tell."